There Was an Old Lady
Who Swallowed a Trout!

for Betty Huffmon and for my daughter, Becky
—T. S.

for Rebecca, Alex, Ranger, Seth, and Theo
—R. R.

SQUARE
FISH

Imprints of Macmillan
175 Fifth Avenue
New York, New York 10010
mackids.com

Henry Holt® is a registered trademark of Henry Holt and Company, LLC. *Publishers since 1866.*
Square Fish and the Square Fish logo are trademarks of Macmillan and
are used by Henry Holt and Company under license from Macmillan.

Library of Congress Cataloging-in-Publication Data
Sloat, Teri. There was an old lady who swallowed a trout / text by Teri Sloat ;
illustrations by Reynold Ruffins. Summary : Set on the coast of the Pacific Northwest, this variation on
the traditional cumulative rhyme describes the silly consequences of an old woman's fishy diet. [1. Marine
animals—Fiction. 2. Northwest, Pacific—Fiction. 3. Nonsense verses.] I. Ruffins, Reynold, ill. II. Title.
PZ8.3.S633136Th   1998   [E]—dc21   98-00607

Originally published in the United States by Henry Holt and Company
First Square Fish Edition : May 2013
Typography by Meredith Baldwin
Square Fish logo designed by Filomena Tuosto

ISBN 978-0-8050-4294-8 (Henry Holt hardcover)
25 24 23 22 21 20 19

ISBN 978-0-8050-6900-6 (Square Fish paperback)
20 19 18

AR : 3.1

There Was an Old Lady
Who Swallowed a Trout!

Teri Sloat

illustrated by Reynold Ruffins

SQUARE
FISH

Henry Holt and Company • New York

There was an old lady who swallowed a trout
That splished and splashed and thrashed about.

It wanted *out!*

There was an old lady who swallowed a salmon
That slippity-flippity-flopped as it swam in.

She swallowed the salmon to catch the trout

That splished and splashed
and thrashed about.
It wanted *out!*

There was an old lady who swallowed an otter.
With a mug of clear water, she swallowed the otter.

She swallowed the otter to catch the salmon;
She swallowed the salmon to catch the trout
That splished and splashed and thrashed about.

It wanted *out!*

There was an old lady who swallowed a seal.
She let out a squeal when she swallowed the seal.

She swallowed the seal to catch the otter;
She swallowed the otter to catch the salmon;
She swallowed the salmon to catch the trout
That splished and splashed and thrashed about.

It wanted *out!*

There was an old lady who swallowed a porpoise.

She did it on purpose; she swallowed the porpoise.

She swallowed the porpoise to catch the seal;
She swallowed the seal to catch the otter;
She swallowed the otter to catch the salmon;
She swallowed the salmon to catch the trout
That splished and splashed and thrashed about.

It wanted *out!*

There was an old lady who swallowed a walrus.
With a great deal of fuss, she swallowed the walrus.

She swallowed the walrus to catch the porpoise;
She swallowed the porpoise to catch the seal;
She swallowed the seal to catch the otter;
She swallowed the otter to catch the salmon;
She swallowed the salmon to catch the trout
That splished and splashed and thrashed about.

It wanted *out!*

There was an old lady who swallowed a whale.
From its tip to its tail, she swallowed that whale.

She swallowed the whale to catch the walrus;
She swallowed the walrus to catch the porpoise;
She swallowed the porpoise to catch the seal;
She swallowed the seal to catch the otter;
She swallowed the otter to catch the salmon;
She swallowed the salmon to catch the trout
That splished and splashed and thrashed about.

It wanted *out!*

There was an old lady who swallowed the ocean.
What a commotion! She swallowed the ocean!

She swallowed the ocean to hold the whale
That now had plenty of room for its tail.
She swallowed the whale to catch the walrus;
She swallowed the walrus to catch the porpoise;
She swallowed the porpoise to catch the seal;
She swallowed the seal to catch the otter;
She swallowed the otter to catch the salmon;
She swallowed the salmon to catch the trout
That splished and splashed and thrashed about.

It wanted *out!*

The old lady started to wriggle and jiggle;
The swirling inside made her hiccup and giggle.
It made her laugh; it made her shout,
And when the old lady opened her mouth . . .

She let out the ocean, the whale, and the walrus,
She let out the porpoise she'd swallowed on purpose;
The seal, the otter, the salmon and trout,
Splished and splashed and thrashed about,

And they all swam

OUT!